# STRATEGIC
## SEARCHES USING
## DIGITAL TOOLS

ISOBEL TOWNE AND JASON PORTERFIELD

rosen publishing's
rosen
central®

New York

Published in 2016 by The Rosen Publishing Group, Inc.
29 East 21st Street, New York, NY 10010

## Library of Congress Cataloging-in-Publication Data

Towne, Isobel, author.
 Strategic searches using digital tools / Isobel Towne and Jason Porterfield. – First edition.
     pages cm. – (Digital and information literacy)
 Audience: Grades 5 to 8.
 Includes bibliographical references and index.
 ISBN 978-1-4994-3791-1 (library bound) – ISBN 978-1-4994-3789-8 (pbk.)
 – ISBN 978-1-4994-3790-4 (6-pack)
 1. Database searching–Juvenile literature. 2. Search engines–Juvenile literature.
 3. Information retrieval–Juvenile literature. I. Porterfield, Jason, author. II. Title. III.
 Series: Digital and information literacy.
 ZA4460.T69 2016
 025.5'24–dc23
                                                                    2015020128

Manufactured in the United States of America

# CONTENTS

# INTRODUCTION

These days it seems like the Internet is everywhere. All we need is some wifi, and we're connected to the World Wide Web to text, post, and e-mail; play games; and catch up on the latest news from anywhere in the world—sometimes as it is happening. Lots of people log onto the Internet to do research. And to access that information, there are search engines. Although e-mail and social media websites are very popular uses of the Internet, sources say that research is always among the most widespread uses.

But a simple search using one word can bring up millions of results. Sometimes that's simply too much information. With billions of web pages available on the World Wide Web, and more being created all the time, wading through thousands, millions, or more of pages to find the most useful or up-to-date information can be overwhelming, especially for first-time or new Internet users. Without an exact web address—called a URL, short for "uniform resource locator"—even well-seasoned Internet users can become frustrated in no time. Luckily, anyone can learn how to use a search engine.

In short, a search engine could be called a major website that has the ability to guide researchers to various web pages and access points like directories and community sites at the same time. The first search engines were developed and organized by specific topics developed to assist users as they searched the web.

Sitting down at the computer to do some research can be a little daunting. By learning the ins and outs of Internet searching and search engines, you can make research a lot more fun and efficient.

There's seemingly no end to the variety of results a search engine can offer a researcher. Some are simply basic documents based on data the search engine has collected.

Search engines also have the ability to incorporate subject directories that are included at the request of the website's creators. But sometimes results come up just because companies or individuals have paid the search engine to include their website among the top of the list. Sometimes returns are made up of information that is screened by people. Other times, however, computer programs may also automatically screen it. And these screens may be based on how popular a site is and data routinely uploaded from online publications like newspapers, magazines, and journals. And even when it seems like a search has been successful, users have to be wary of which links they click.

Some search engines are better for specific kinds of searches. They might search a number of other search engines, yielding plenty of results. However, sometimes their investigation is rather shallow.

This instructive volume is here to help take some of the mystery out of online researching. Users will learn how to make the most of their search, using specific terms, phrases, symbols, and more. They'll learn about all of the different kinds of search engines and how to use them to their best advantage, making time at the keyboard useful as well as enjoyable. Get ready to search.

# Chapter 1

# The Essentials of Search Engines

**W**hen it comes right down to it, search engines are a lot like the card catalog in your local library. They are basically humongous databases.

Think about this: One search for a phrase such as "running tips" could bring up millions of results, but the search engine, no matter which one it is, did not even search the whole Internet. What it did do was search web pages and websites that it previously cataloged and collected.

Every search engine works a little differently. No matter which one, however, its

What might seem like a simple search can end up collecting millions of results, causing no small amount of frustration.

work is made up of three essential parts: a crawler, an indexer, and the query process.

## Spiders, Robots, and Worms

Crawlers—sometimes called spiders, robots, or worms—are computer programs that visit web pages, download all of the information on those pages, and then follow links to other pages within the website. They then send this information on to the search engine's indexer.

There are two ways that crawlers find information. In the early days of the Internet, people could add their sites to search engine databases. Unfortunately, some users abused this method by sending fake posts, forcing search engine companies to phase out that method of notification. Today, crawlers look at the URL links on web pages automatically and then review them to screen out any bogus links.

Along with analyzing and indexing information, the crawler makes other refinements to the information it gathers before it becomes available to Internet users. Crawlers detect and remove spam pages (pages that falsely feature search terms to get users to visit them), find and delete duplicate pages, and also do some quality testing on search terms and results.

All of this makes crawling the Internet very expensive for search companies, so most set a limit on the number of pages on a website that a crawler may visit. These websites remain un-indexed, and while the potentially valuable information on them is still available to users, it is harder to find than indexed information.

The time that it takes for crawlers to index web pages can be a drawback to using search engines to find up-to-date information. Some crawlers can index millions of web pages a day, but the vast size of the Internet sometimes causes delays between the time information goes up on the web and the time that a crawler finds it. Many search engine companies claim that their crawlers are constantly looking for the most recent information available, but some studies have shown that these companies are often weeks behind in re-crawling and indexing material.

## Collect, Classify, and Categorize

The indexer is the part of the search engine that collects, classifies, and categorizes all of the information the crawler finds. Until a search engine indexes a web page, that page remains unavailable to people using the search engine. Once the web page is indexed, any changes that are later made to the web page are updated in the index so that the changes can be reflected in searches.

A web page is logged and then stored in the search engine's database by the indexer. This allows the search engine to expand its search beyond keyword searches and find words that are close to each other, usually through the advanced search options offered by many search engines. Some search engines also index the coding of websites, enabling the search engine to look by using web page categories, such as titles or even URLs.

The indexing is done by a software program, and indexers use mathematical formulas to calculate the rankings of returns for the search terms entered. Many indexers eliminate common words that do not impact search results, such as "and," "for," and "is," from the search engine's database to make the search engine perform more efficiently. Some search engine indexers also eliminate punctuation marks and change letters to make the search engine work faster.

## High-Profile Search Engines

Ever since the Internet became available for public use, hundreds of search engines have been created. Many more have either been discontinued or absorbed by larger companies or remain obscure. Others have existed for years.

AltaVista was one of the first search engines that made people sit up and take notice around 1995. AltaVista was easy to use, fast, and large. Its advanced search options allowed users to perform very precise searches through phrase searches, by highlighting keywords, and even by using case-sensitive matches to find words with uppercase letters. After being bought and sold to various companies from 1998 onward, this stalwart search engine held on until it just couldn't keep up. In 2013, its final owner, Yahoo!, retired AltaVista for good.

Yahoo! began in 1994 as a directory, which categorizes information rather than searches for it, and now uses its own crawler to perform searches. Yahoo! allows searches in other languages and returns results that include maps and images. Yahoo! has a sizable list of shortcuts that allow users to quickly find data ranging from local temperatures to driving directions.

Live Search was a search site owned and operated by software giant Microsoft. Live Search offered several innovative features, such as allowing users to scroll through additional search results on the same page rather than having to keep clicking on pages to see results. In 2009, Microsoft retired Live Search and presented the search engine Bing. Microsoft called Bing a "decision engine" because it was intended to show more information in its search results so that users could make better decisions about which link to click. In 2015, Bing's video search was rolled out and widely lauded as being more effective than Google's or YouTube's video search.

There are some "newer" search engines that have more of a visual approach to searching, such as EyeIn, KartOO, and Ask.

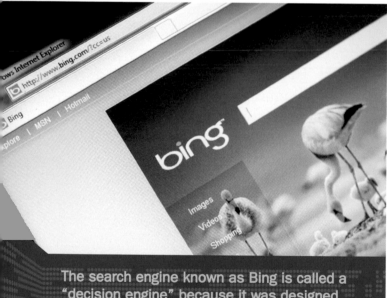

The search engine known as Bing is called a "decision engine" because it was designed with the idea that it would show search results that would facilitate decision making.

Meanwhile, new and innovative search engines are always being developed. For example, the search engine Xirkle offers web, video, and job search options.

The search engine Google initially launched in 1998 and quickly became so popular that the word "google" itself became synonymous with searching for information online. It is now the largest and most popular search engine. Google ranks websites by popularity, basing its rankings on what other pages link or refer to it, and tends to find pages that other users have visited recently.

Today, Google is far more than a search engine. It now offers a highly developed mapping system, allows users to share their documents online, and even allows users to search inside books that have been electronically scanned into a database. While other search engines may offer some of these features, none is currently as comprehensive as Google. It even developed Google Glass, a wearable computer that allows users to search maps and the Internet, as well as other fun options. Unfortunately, as of early 2015, Google announced it was going to discontinue sales of the would-be cutting-edge search technology so it could concentrate on future evolutions.

One of Google's more interesting inventions has been Google Glass, a wearable computer that allows users to do many things, including searching the Internet and maps.

## Ask Me a Question

The query process that search engines use is the final and most complex part of the search engine. For search engine users, the query process is fairly simple. Users type their search terms into a part of the search engine's web page called a field and click on a button to see results. Today's search engines work extremely quickly, seldom giving users time to wonder how they gather information before displaying a page of results ranked by how relevant they are to the search terms.

In the seconds it takes for a search engine to return results, the search engine is evaluating all of the web pages in its database using all kinds of different factors and sets of mathematical rules called algorithms to figure out what pages are relevant. The exact process varies among search engines, and search engine companies closely guard the algorithms they use to figure out what pages are relevant and rank the results.

Algorithms are considered trade secrets by search engine companies. However, there are a few general rules that most search engines still follow. One rule of ranking is where keywords are placed on a page, as well as how often they show up on a web page. Search engines will consider web pages that include the search terms in their "title tag," or heading, at the top of the screen to be more relevant to the search terms than other pages. This is also a fact for web pages with frequently used search terms, because this makes it appear as though the page has more apt information compared to other pages. There are even search engines that can look for common search phrases, such as movie titles, based on preprogrammed results.

# MYTHS & FACTS

**MYTH** The Internet is the same thing as the web.

**FACT** Although you can click your way to millions of sites that use the same procedures to exchange information, the World Wide Web is only a small part of the whole Internet.

**MYTH** One search engine will get me the same information as any other.

**FACT** These days there are all kinds of search engines, and many operate in different ways, whether it's how they sort information or how that information is presented on the page.

**MYTH** The most important information in a search engine appears in the links close to the top of the search engine's return page.

**FACT** Some companies pay money to search engines to get their web pages to show up at or close to the top.

# Chapter 2

# First Step: Word Searches

Keyword searches are used by every search engine. The user types in the words to look up information. The most basic kind of search involves typing one word into the search field. The user clicks "search" and views the results. The danger of this method is that one general word can yield thousands or even millions of links to information. For example, keying the term "mythology" into the Google search box results in more than 64 million links. Some link to pages about Greek mythology, while other results range from books one can buy about mythology to online gaming.

To avoid creating this kind of situation, users should first have a good idea of exactly what kind of information they want to find. This will allow the user to come up with good search terms. Since "mythology" is far too broad a search term, the searcher may want to add other key words to the search.

As the search becomes more specific, results will also become more refined. Typing "mythological gods" into the search field narrows the search to more than one million, and more of those results will focus on information

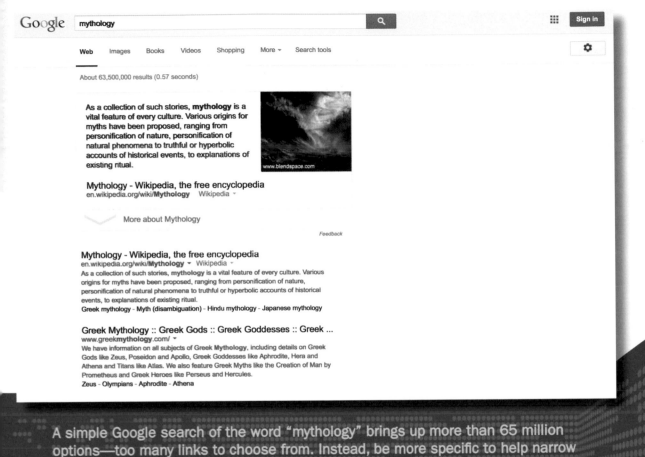

A simple Google search of the word "mythology" brings up more than 65 million options—too many links to choose from. Instead, be more specific to help narrow down the search.

about mythology. Typing in the name of a specific god will bring down the number of results. For example, "mythological god Apollo" has about 336,000 results.

## Getting Specific

Three hundred thousand web pages that mention the god Apollo are still far too many for a single person to read. Deciding which of these web pages to look at can be tricky. While many of the web pages listed in the results may contain accurate information from good sources, others may be incorrect, misleading, or completely irrelevant.

Most search engines today provide a few lines of text showing the context in which the search term was used, and users can often figure out whether or not a website will be useful from those lines of text. If the text is written in a language that the user can't read, it probably won't be very useful unless the search engine has a translation feature. It will also probably be obvious if the search term is being used in a work of fiction, a joke, or a context that is completely opposite from what the user needs.

---

File    Edit    View    Favorites    Tools    Help

`ONLINE PUBLIC INFORMATION`

## Online Public Information

When looking for a great source for raw material for research projects, head to public records. These might be Federal Bureau of Investigation (FBI) files about dead celebrities or local zoning laws. Often, this sort of information is easily obtained online by searching government sites for local, state, and federal information. Even if a local government doesn't have the documents available online, their website may tell you where to find them. For many federal and state government agencies, you may be able to fill out a Freedom of Information Act request for the documents online. The Freedom of Information Act is a federal law guaranteeing a citizen's right to government information, and it allows citizens to request government documents. Remember that some government information—facts that may compromise national security or violate a citizen's privacy—are not subject to the law. Also, some information on documents may be blocked out by the agency and therefore difficult to read and not very much help in a search.

Of course, even the best information sometimes goes out of date as events transpire or more facts are uncovered. When dealing with the sciences, politics, current events, or any number of other topics, information can change daily or even hourly, and it is important to get the latest data. Fortunately, many websites linked with journals, magazines, and other publications sort their articles by date or even by time posted, offering the most recent items on the site's first page. Older articles are often stored in a database, which users can search. Some websites for individuals or organizations may not keep their information quite so fresh, though they may let the user know when the site was last updated.

Looking for a list of links to other websites can quickly expand the range of results from a word search. Usually, a links page will offer a brief description of the site so that users can decide if it will be relevant to them. Some of these links may offer information on topics that are closely related to the search terms. A website about the pirate Blackbeard, for example, may have a link to another site about life in coastal towns during the eighteenth century. Links like these can often help a user gain perspective on his or her topic.

## Categories of Websites

Normally, websites can be placed into six different categories: advocacy, business, informational, news, personal, and entertainment. Advocacy sites exist to influence public opinion or to promote a cause or a nonprofit organization. Business sites generally promote a product or service. Informational sites exist to provide factual information to the public. News sites offer information about local, regional, national, or international news. Personal sites usually offer information about an individual, such as his or her interests. Entertainment sites simply exist to entertain.

## Determining Domain Names and URLs

One way to determine if search results are helpful is to look at the URL, which stands for uniform resource locator, for the web pages that have been returned. Every website on the Internet has a URL, which enables Internet users to easily access websites that are hosted by different servers through the web browser. Part of the URL contains the domain name, which consists of two parts. The first part of the domain name often identifies the organization, while the second part, called the generic top-level domain, tells the user what sort of organization it is.

There are five generic domain names currently in use in the United States: .gov, .com, .net, .edu, and .org, as well as several others that are not used as frequently. Some experts in Internet research rank the relevance of websites based on the domain name.

Sites tagged .edu and .k12 are often considered trustworthy because they are used for college and university sites. College and university web pages may include a host of information from various academic departments, from the results of research projects to background information on famous alumni or even copies of documents owned by the school's library. Still, some college departments may be lax in updating the information on their sites. Also, students and even staff members may post incorrect information online.

Federal government departments use the .gov and .mil domain names. The many departments and bureaus using .gov range from the FBI to the Library of Congress. Web pages for government bureaus often contain raw data, such as census numbers, and a brief abstract explaining what the numbers mean. Congressional websites may have information about legislation under consideration or laws that have already been passed. Some government websites may also post information on how various government bureaus work or offer tips for the public. Many even offer a form for users to request government documents using the Freedom of Information Act.

Websites that use the other three domain names often require more scrutiny. Sites that use .org are often nonprofit organizations. These groups are usually committed to a specific agenda and are interested in sharing information about what they do. They can range widely from public library

The Library of Congress (https://www.loc.gov) is just one of many reputable government (.gov) websites. The LOC is the world's biggest library with millions of books, recordings, photographs, maps, and manuscripts in its collections.

websites to nationwide conservation groups to local church groups. Some of these sites may provide a great deal of accurate information, while others say very little. With these sites, it is often a good idea to double-check information against information found in other sources, as the information may be politically biased. Also look for contact information and a list of web links on the website, both of which may provide information about the people running the site and the accuracy of their information.

Commercial websites tend to use .com domains. Expect to find a diverse range of information on such sites. Some may be educational or the websites of trustworthy newspapers or magazines, such as the *New York Times* or *National Geographic* magazine. Some websites may include inaccurate data or even be intentionally erroneous. Keep an eye out for the names of dependable companies or recognized experts in the field. Carefully examine any links. Always verify the information gathered from these sites. Websites that use .net are typically Internet networks. These sites need to be examined with care, too.

# Chapter 3

# Tactics for Advanced Searches

hen a one-word keyword search results in far too many links to make sense of, it's time to do a more refined search. Anyone can check out online subject directories to locate more specific websites. When a search seems like a dead end, a wildcard may help develop a search. Should the problem be a glut of information, a user can adjust the search terms so that they are more precise, or a phrase search might offer more exact results.

## Searching by Phrase

Phrase searches consist of a phrase placed inside double quotation marks. This tells the search engine to search for the exact phrase within the quotation marks. Instead of looking for search terms in any order, as they would with an ordinary word search, search engines take the terms placed in double quotes and search for them in that exact order.

Phrase searches often drastically reduce the number of returns by eliminating web pages that do not have the terms in the exact order. They are particularly useful if a user is looking for a quote from a speech, the title of a book, or a full name. Phrase searches also can be used alongside ordinary word searches to help focus a search or alongside other phrases.

While phrase searches can sometimes help a user find specific information more quickly, there are pitfalls. Spelling can sometimes be a problem with phrase searches, as the smallest typing mistake when entering search terms can prevent a user from seeing helpful sites. Phrase searches may help to narrow the list of returns, but in some cases, they may also prevent possibly useful sites from coming up.

## Linked Search Terms and Symbols

Boolean operators are words that can be used to link search terms together to help narrow or broaden a search. The most common Boolean operators are the words "and," "or," and "not." These words are sometimes capitalized and are coded into the search engine's

Thanks to the work of English mathematician George Boole (1815–1864), we can now use Boolean operators to connect search terms for a more specific Internet search.

software to let the search engine know that it's supposed to perform a particular function when they are used.

For example, using the search terms "camera AND instructions" will narrow the search by telling the search engine that the user is looking for articles or web pages using both terms. "Camera OR darkroom" broadens the search by telling the search engine to find sites that include either term. Using "camera NOT digital" weeds out pages that are irrelevant to the user by indicating that the search engine should leave out sites that use the second word. Boolean operators also may be represented by symbols. The "+" sign indicates the word "AND," while the "-" sign indicates "NOT."

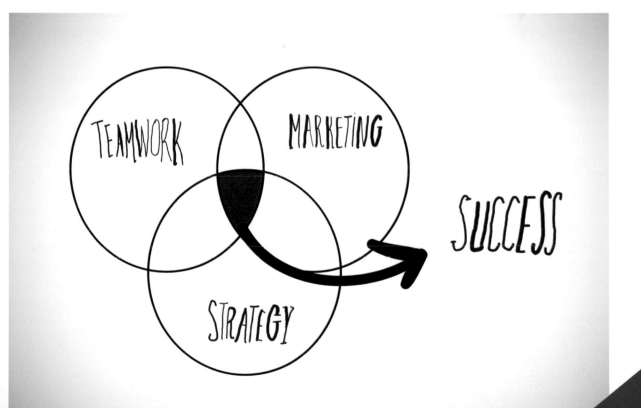

Venn diagrams can help explain Boolean logic. For example, a search can be narrowed using the word AND. Use OR for a broader search, or narrow it just a little by using the word NOT to link two terms.

Symbols are also used in word-stemming searches. In word-stemming searches, the user types only part of a word and inserts a symbol—often called a wildcard—to represent the untyped part, often at the end of a word. The symbol tells the search engine to look for variations on a word, rather than just searching for the word itself. Often, the symbol used is "*," but some search engines may use other symbols, such as "$," "!," or "#." With the wildcard, a user could type "pirate*" to tell the search engine to look for pirate as well as "pirates," "pirated," and "piratical." Wildcards therefore let users broaden their searches without having to type in all of the words they wanted to find.

The wildcard feature has to be specially designed into the search engine, a costly process. While many search engines that were started in the 1990s had this feature at one point, many have dropped it. However, wildcards are not entirely a thing of the past. The advanced search option on the search engine Google allows users to search using wildcards, and the function is used by many online resources, such as dictionaries and databases.

## Getting Advanced with Searches

Most search engines have built-in features for expanding or narrowing searches. Usually one reaches them by clicking on an "advanced search" link on the search engine's site. Advanced search pages often have separate fields for exact phrase searches. Other fields let users enter combinations of search terms, broadening the search by looking for alternate words.

Advanced searches may also let users search for websites in other languages. While this may seem helpful only if a user can read the language, some major sites—such as those connected to governments or universities—offer translated versions through links on their pages. Also, some search engines have translation features that allow users to see a translated version of the web page. Search engine translation features have limitations—translations may not cover all of the text on the page and are performed by computer programs, which can lead to imprecise word choices—but they can be useful if a user wants to see what an expert who speaks another language says or if he or she is interested in examining a topic from another culture's point of view.

Advanced search pages may have fields that allow users to type in words to exclude from the search. This feature can be helpful if a set of search terms keeps bringing up unwanted pages. For example, a user looking for websites about pirates may want to exclude the words "sports" or "ball" to direct the search away from sites about sports mascots. Some advanced search options on search engines like Google are set up to allow users to look for a specific word within a specific URL.

File    Edit    View    Favorites    Tools    Help

WIKI WEBSITES AND WEBLOGS

## Wiki Websites and Weblogs

In the last few years, wiki sites and blogs have exploded in popularity. On a wiki site the information is regarded as based on fact, and users can log on and contribute content to web pages or edit content that is already in place. Weblogs, better known as blogs, usually serve as online diaries, giving readers insight into the lives, thoughts, and opinions of their authors. Blogs began in the late 1990s and have become so mainstream that many news sites now have blog features written by journalists, and some independent blogs are considered trustworthy news sources. There are now specialized search tools designed just for searching blogs. Wikis began at about the same time as a way to let ordinary people share their knowledge on the Internet. One of the best-known wiki sites is Wikipedia, an online encyclopedia compiled through input from users. While both blogs and wiki sites may present factual information, users should be very careful about taking information from them unless it can be checked against other sources.

# Website Databases

Subject directories are databases of websites and online documents organized by category, much like the Yellow Pages or business listings in a phone book. Just as a Yellow Pages user would look under the heading "restaurants" to find a pizza parlor nearby, subject directory users look under subject headings to find information on specific topics. They are usually incorporated within major search engines, but unlike search engines themselves, the categorization is performed by humans rather than computer programs. Results are returned in a series of menus arranged by subject. The search engine Yahoo! started out as a subject directory and still has an extensive subject directory. For example, users planning to visit a particular city can look that city up in the subject directory and then use it to find hotels, restaurants, museums, or other attractions.

Search engines try to rank the most relevant results first, while subject directories are organized in categories. These are usually presented alphabetically, and category titles may differ from one directory to the next. Subject directories take a great deal of effort to launch because people organize, evaluate, and catalog the information using predetermined criteria and then arrange, annotate, and code it. Therefore, their databases are usually much smaller than those of the search engines. They often make up for this by supplementing their results with results from search engine partners such as Google.

Subject directories can be great tools, particularly if a user is just getting started on a search. Users can use directory categories to help shape future searches, narrowing a general topic to more specific search terms. Results from subject directories are often very relevant to a general topic, since the pages in the directories are cataloged by people who evaluate them for their value to a topic.

However, there are also disadvantages. Because the subject directory databases are much smaller than those of search engines, users don't get as many returns on a search. Users also may not get the most up-to-date results possible when using subject directories. There can be a significant time lag between the time that a page is published and the time it is entered into subject directories. While directory results are often highly relevant to search terms, many of the pages may be out of date—sometimes by years— even before they are evaluated and cataloged in the database.

## The Marvels of Metasearch Engines

Metasearch engines are search engines that collect the results of other search engines. Essentially, this means that they search the indexes of multiple search engines at once. In other words, they plug your search terms into other search tools and bring back the results. On the surface, they work just like a regular search engine. A user types search terms into a field and clicks on a button telling it to find information. They extract what they interpret to

To get a general feel for what information might be available on a topic that is new to you, consider using a metasearch engine, which collects results from other search engines.

be the most relevant results and return those to the user. Popular metasearch engines include Ixquick Metasearch, Dogpile, and Yippy.

Metasearch engines can be tremendous time savers because they can go through several search engines at once. They can be very helpful to users who are trying to get a general feel for what information is available online on a particular topic. They are also useful for finding a large number of results on a particular subject, searching the entire text of multiple documents, and for users with narrow or obscure research topics. Metasearch engines can also search the web for particular types of documents, file types, source locations, or even for most recently updated documents.

Metasearch engines sometimes take a longer time to do their work. The delay makes sense when you think about how they are sifting through data from multiple databases. Major search engines, such as Google, might deny a metasearch engine access, so sometimes their results are incomplete. Search terms might be extremely simplified as a way to speed the search process. They may only search a small party of each search engine's database. And because they are only gathering the first few links from each specific search engine, be aware that their results might be a bit slanted. In other words, search results might be overwhelmingly from sites that are listed at the top of a results page because they pay for that placement. But remember that both subject directories and conventional search engines are out there to make money. Either way, they receive money in exchange for listing particular websites closer to the top of their results.

# TEN GREAT QUESTIONS

## TO ASK AN INFORMATION SPECIALIST

1   What is the most efficient way to search the Internet for publicly available documents?

2   What do you recommend as the best way to decide which websites are related to my topic?

3   What do you suggest is a good approximate number of web pages to review and verify my information before I find what I'm looking for?

4   How do I decide whether or not I can trust a website?

5   What kinds of websites have the best information for my topic?

6   What's a good way to come up with useful search terms that will help me focus my research?

7   Can you suggest search engine tips and shortcuts that will help me both quickly and accurately find the information I am looking for?

8   How do I use the advanced search options on a search engine's web page?

9   When do I know that I have a sufficient amount of information on the topic I am researching?

10   If I want more specific results, what Internet resources are available for helping me refine my search?

# Chapter 4

# Concluding the Search

I t may seem like search engines are a snap to use. Some people type in some search terms, scan the first page results, and just click on the top sources without taking much time to check them out. Other people are the opposite. They may spend quite a bit of time perusing pages of results without coming up with satisfactory information.

## Website Assessment

Chapter 2 touched on some quick and basic ways that a search engine user can quickly evaluate the usefulness of a website. However, even if the website appears to be valuable on the surface, the user should still look deeper to evaluate the information that he or she receives. Users should look at the website and judge its accuracy, authority, objectivity, coverage, and whether or not the information is timely. The timeliness of information is known as currency.

# News Online

In the early days of the Internet, few would have imagined that millions of people would someday read the news online. Many newspapers, television networks, and radio stations now post and update their stories online and

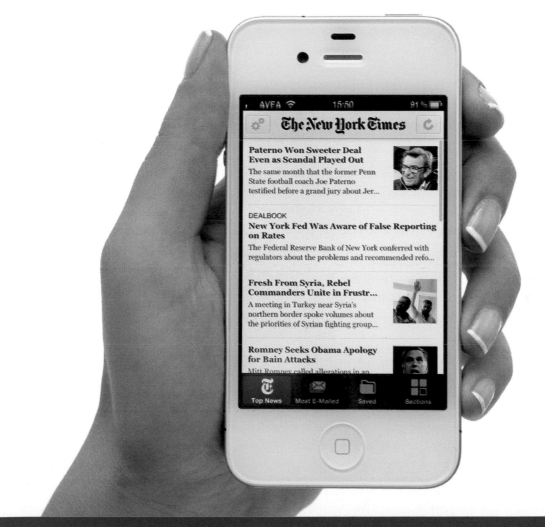

The *New York Times* is just one of many well-known, high-profile newspapers that allow users to search stories and up-to-the-minute news. Magazines and broadcast news networks also have searchable web pages.

are gradually moving toward creating original content for the web only, responding to "nontraditional" news outlets that are based solely online. Journalism organizations have also responded to the growing trend over the years, posting tips for researching, writing, and developing content online, from how to post sound and video clips to how to remain current in the constant news cycle of today's world.

## Cross-Check It

Often, the fastest way to confirm accuracy is to check the information against other sources. If the information on a website contradicts other current sources, there's a good chance that it's incorrect. Users should always be careful to check information found on the Internet against other sources, such as posted links to other pages and articles and, if possible, sources that are not online, such as authoritative books, encyclopedias, or periodicals.

Also check for grammatical errors and spelling mistakes. Even if a site originates from a trusted source, the information may not have been double-checked for accuracy before being posted online. If the web page offers a research document or the results of a study, look for an explanation of how the data was collected and interpreted. If there is any doubt that the information on a web page is inaccurate, the user should leave it out.

It is also important to remember that just because several websites have the same information doesn't mean that information is accurate. Many web pages "mirror" information from other pages, meaning that they simply post the same information without checking it thoroughly for accuracy. This sometimes leads to the spread of inaccurate information and increases the importance of using other sources, such as books, to cross-check information. For example, a Google search for "Burmese mountain dog" will return about 898,000 hits, even though the breed's name is actually spelled "Burnese mountain dog."

If something about a website seems suspect, carefully scan for spelling and grammar mistakes. Always verify information against one or more other reputable sites, even if the site seems trustworthy.

# Getting Reputable

Always look for information about a web page's author or sponsor to help judge whether or not the information can be trusted. While anyone may write about a topic, it's always best to use information from people with certified qualifications. Look on the site for references to other publications from the page's author, as well as background information like work experience in the field, degrees, and affiliations with respected organizations. If the site does not list the people responsible for the information presented, check to see if the site was sponsored by an authoritative organization or entity.

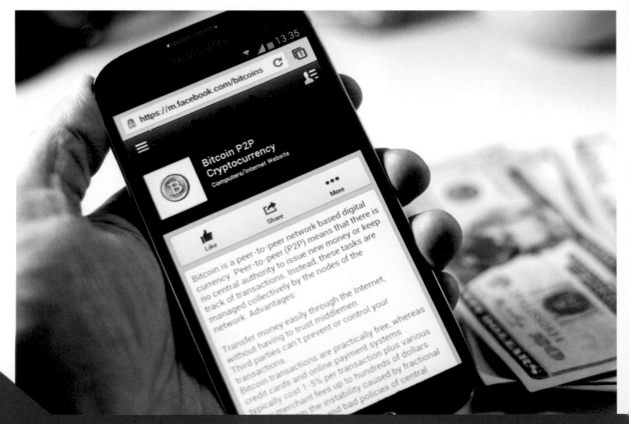

A good place to get a sense of the focus and aims of a website is to check out the section that is often called "About Us."

# Neutrality

Authors always have personal points of view. How much they allow their own feelings or beliefs to show may help a user decide whether or not their web pages are useful. Journalists often try to present both sides of a story, and academic writers use arguments that cite the work of other scholars. Look for sites that present two sides of an argument or story. These perspectives show that the author did enough research to show a basic understanding of a topic's many facets.

Avoid information from controversial authors who may not present both sides or who don't cite their sources. These may be opinion pieces, and while the information within may be factual, there are likely to be many other sources that present the same information in a more scholarly way. However, there may be cases where it is necessary to use biased information in order to present both sides of the argument. In these cases, check the facts used in the pages, make it clear that the information is biased, and clarify what information might be inaccurate.

## Attention to Detail

Coverage deals with the amount of information presented on a website and how many details it covers. A website may be too general for the topic a user is researching or too detailed in aspects that are irrelevant to the search. Users should judge if a website presents specific information that fits the needs of their research or whether it is too broad or too narrow to use.

## Is It Current?

Currency refers to the timeliness of the information posted. As explained in chapter 2, users should check how often a site is updated or if the site indicates when the last update was performed. While it may not matter how often a site is updated for some topics, for others, it is important to get the most up-to-date information. Some web pages actually include dates showing the last time a page was updated.

# Keeping the Search in Check

The size and sprawling nature of the Internet makes it possible to find information on nearly any subject. At the same time, it may also prove distracting. For some searches, hundreds or thousands of web pages may be returned. While it's important to try to be thorough when doing research, it's also important to avoid getting bogged down in sites that may not be relevant.

One way users can avoid this is to have a clear idea of exactly what kind of information they need. Be as specific as possible with search terms to ensure that the pages most relevant to a topic are returned. If using multiple search engines, be sure to avoid visiting links that you've already seen. Also, remain focused on your goal. Search engines sometimes turn up irrelevant results. While some of these may be interesting, there's no point in spending a lot of time looking at them if they don't say anything about the search topic.

Because many search engines list links by their relevance, it is usually not necessary—and sometimes not possible—to go through all of them. Typically, returns become less relevant to the search terms used as you go down the list. To save time, you may want to concentrate on just the first few pages of returns. If there is nothing useful in the first few pages, it may be necessary to change the search terms.

It's also a good idea to limit search sessions to a certain time frame. Search for a while, and then do something else before returning to the search. Looking at web pages can be tiring, and taking breaks from the search will help keep your mind fresh for evaluating web pages.

# GLOSSARY

**algorithm** A step-by-step process for solving a problem or finishing a task.

**blog** A shared online journal used by people to post their insights and information about their lives, interests, and experiences.

**Boolean** Relating to a mathematical system of notation invented in the nineteenth century that symbolically shows relationships between things and that has been applied to the web by using the words "and," "not," and "or" to narrow or broaden searches.

**browser** A software program used to access the Internet in order to view documents.

**catalog** A complete list of items or information, usually arranged systematically.

**category** A collection of things that share something in common, as in topics in subject directories.

**database** An organized body of related information.

**directory** A listing of stored information.

**domain name** The part of a URL (web address) that usually specifies the organization and type of organization and where a web page is located.

**Freedom of Information Act** A law stating that every executive-branch government agency must publish instructions on how the public can get information from the agency.

**Internet** A worldwide network of computer networks that all use the same protocols to exchange data.

**link** An instruction that connects one part of a program or an element on a list to another program or list.

**metasearch engines** Search services that search several individual search engines at once and then combine the results.

**network** A system of interconnected computers that exchange data.

**program** A sequence of instructions that a computer can interpret and execute.

**relevance** The degree to which websites found are judged to be useful.

**search engine** A software tool that allows web users to find information on the network.

**server** A computer that provides clients with access to files and printers as part of a shared network.

**software** Written programs or procedures or rules relating to the operation of a computer system.

**subject directory** Collections of high-quality web pages organized into subject categories by people, often librarians or subject specialists.

**URL** Acronym for uniform resource locator, the address by which a web page can be located on the web.

The Freedom of Information Act (FOIA)
FOIA Officer
National Telecommunications and Information Administration
U.S. Department of Commerce
14th Street and Constitution Avenue, N.W., Room 4713
Washington, DC 20230
E-mail: eFOIA@ntia.doc.gov
Website: https://foiaonline.regulations.gov/foia/action/public/home
To make your own Freedom of Information Act (FOIA) request or to research
other requests that have been made previously, head to the FOIA
website.

Internet Society
1775 Wiehle Avenue, Suite 201
Reston, VA 20190-5108
(703) 439-2120
E-mail: isoc@isoc.org
Website: http://www.internetsociety.org/
The Internet Society was founded in 1992 to provide leadership in Internet-
related standards, education, and policy around the world.

Media Smarts
950 Gladstone Avenue, Suite 120
Ottawa, ON K1Y 3E6
Canada
(613) 224-7721; (800) 896-3342 (North America)
E-mail: info@mediasmarts.ca
Website: http://mediasmarts.ca/

This organization, formerly Media Awareness Network, offers resources and
support for anyone interested in media and information literacy for
young people.

National Telecommunications and Information Administration
1401 Constitution Avenue, NW
Washington, DC 20230
(202) 482-2000
Website: http://www.ntia.doc.gov/
The National Telecommunications and Information Administration (NTIA)
advises the president on telecommunications and information policy
issues.

People for Internet Responsibility (PFIR)
c/o Peter G. Neumann, Principal Scientist
Computer Science Lab SRI International EL-243
333 Ravenswood Avenue
Menlo Park, CA 94025-3493
(650) 859-2375
E-mail: neumann@pfir.org
Website: http://www.pfir.org
The People for Internet Responsibility (PFIR) organization is a global, grass-
roots, ad hoc network of individuals who are concerned about current
and future operations, development, management, and regulation of
the Internet.

U.S. Internet Service Provider Association
700 12th Street NW, Suite 700E

Washington, DC 20005
(202) 904-2351
E-mail: kdean@usispa.org
Website: http://www.usispa.org
The U.S. Internet Service Provider Association is a group representing the
interests of affiliated Internet service providers.

## Websites

Due to the changing nature of Internet links, Rosen Publishing has developed an online list of websites related to the subject of this book. This site is
updated regularly. Please use this link to access the list:

http://www.rosenlinks.com/DIL/Search

# FOR FURTHER READING

Barker, Donald I., and Melissa S. Barker. *Internet Research: Illustrated.* 7th edition. Stamford, CT: Cengage Learning, 2014.

Bingham, Jane. *Internet Freedom: Where Is the Limit?* Portsmouth, NH: Heinemann Library, 2006.

Endsley, Keiza. *How to Do Great Online Research* (Web Wisdom). New York, NY: Cavendish Square, 2015.

Fontichiaro, Kristin. *Go Straight to the Source* (Explorer Library: Information Explorer). Ann Arbor, MI: Cherry Lake Publishing, 2013.

Fontichiaro, Kristin. *Blog It!* (Explorer Library: Information Explorer). Ann Arbor, MI: Cherry Lake Publishing, 2013.

Fontichiaro, Kristin, and Emily Johnson. *Know What to Ask: Forming Great Research Questions* (Explorer Library: Information Explorer). Ann Arbor, MI: Cherry Lake Publishing, 2013.

Gad, Victor. *The Research Virtuoso: How to Find Anything You Need to Know.* Buffalo, NY: Annick Press, 2012.

Gordon, Sherri. *Downloading Copyrighted Stuff from the Internet: Stealing or Fair Use?* Berkeley Heights, NJ: Enslow Publishers, 2005.

Hawthorn, Kate. *The Young Person's Guide to the Internet.* New York, NY: Routledge, 2005.

Marcovitz, Hal. *Online Information and Research.* San Diego, CA: ReferencePoint Press, 2012.

Newman, Matthew. *You Have Mail: True Stories of Cybercrime.* London, England: Franklin Watts, 2007.

Parks, Peggy. *The Internet.* San Diego, CA: Lucent Books, 2005.

Pascaretti, Vicki, and Sara Wilkie. *Team Up Online: Super Smart Information Strategies* (Information Explorer). Ann Arbor, MI: Cherry Lake Publishing, 2012.

Randolph, Ryan. *New Research Techniques: Getting the Most Out of Search Engine Tools* (Digital and Information Literacy). New York, NY: Rosen Publishing, 2011.

Torr, James. *Opposing Viewpoints: The Internet*. San Diego, CA: Greenhaven Press, 2005.

Truesdale, Ann. *Find the Right Site* (Explorer Library: Information Explorer). Ann Arbor, MI: Cherry Lake Publishing, 2013.

Witten, Ian, Marco Gorl, and Teresa Numerico. *Web Dragons: Inside the Myths of Search Engine Technology*. San Francisco, CA: Morgan Kaufmann, 2006.

# BIBLIOGRAPHY

Ackerman, Earnest, and Karen Hartman. *The Information Searcher's Guide to Searching and Researching on the Internet.* Wilsonville, OR: ABF Content, 2001.

Baylin, Ed. *Effective Internet Search.* Ottawa, Canada: Baylin Systems, Inc., 2005.

BBC News. "Google Glass Sales Halted but Firm Says Kit Is Not Dead." January 15, 2015. Retrieved June 23, 2015 (http://www.bbc.com/news/technology-30831128).

Bilton, Nicky. "Why Google Glass Broke." *New York Times*, February 4, 2015. Retrieved June 23, 2015 (http://www.nytimes.com/2015/02/05/style/why-google-glass-broke.html?_r=1).

Calishain, Tara. *Information Trapping: Real-Time Research on the Web.* Berkeley, CA: New Riders, 2007.

Diaz, Karen, and Nancy O'Hanlon. *IssueWeb: A Guide and Sourcebook for Researching Controversial Issues on the Web.* Westport, CT: Greenwood Publishing Group, Inc., 2004.

Hannon Library. "Internet Searching Tools." Southern Oregon University, July 8, 2014. Retrieved June 23, 2015 (http://hanlib.sou.edu/searchtools/metatool.html).

Hock, Randolph. *The Extreme Searcher's Internet Handbook.* Medford, NJ: CyberAge Books, 2004.

Kraynak, Joe. *Best of the Internet.* Indianapolis, IN: Que Publishing, 2005.

Milstein, Sarah, J. D. Biersdorfer, and Matthew MacDonald. *Google: The Missing Manual.* Cambridge, MA: O'Reilly Media, 2006.

Mintz, Anna, ed. *Web of Deception: Misinformation on the Internet.* Medford, NJ: CyberAge Books, 2002.

Radford, Marie, Susan Barnes, and Linda Barr. *Web Research: Selecting, Evaluating, and Citing.* New York, NY: Pearson Education, Inc., 2006.

Rodriguez, Salvador. "Microsoft's New Bing Video Search: 4 Ways It Beats Google, YouTube." International Business Times, June 22, 2015. Retrieved June 23, 2015 (http://www.ibtimes.com/microsofts-new-bing-video-search-4-ways-it-beats-google-youtube-1978126).

Schlein, Alan. Find It Online: The Complete Guide to Online Research. Tempe, AZ: Facts on Demand Press, 2003.

Sullivan, Danny. "A Eulogy For AltaVista, The Google of Its Time." Search Engine Land, June 28, 2013. Retrieved June 23, 2015 (http://searchengineland.com/altavista-eulogy-165366).

TIME Staff. "Best Inventions of the Year 2012: Google Glass." Time, October 31, 2012. Retrieved June 23, 2015 (http://techland.time.com/2012/11/01/best-inventions-of-the-year-2012/slide/google-glass/).

# INDEX

## About the Author

Isobel Towne is an author and editor specializing in science and philosophy, which require ample online research. She lives on the coast of northern Maine where she can ramble along the rocks.

Jason Porterfield has written more than twenty books for Rosen Publishing on subjects ranging from American history to environmental science.

## Photo Credits